MIKE CARPENTER

VENICE

*Its History, Its Art,
Its Landmarks*

Copyright © 2023 by Mike Carpenter

Cover art © 2023 by Believer
Winged Lion of Venice © 2023 by Nymur Khan
Cover design by Elisa Pinizzotto

All rights reserved. No part of this publication may be reproduced, stored in a retrieval system, or transmitted, in any form or by any means, without the author's prior permission. For all inquiries, including requests for commercial use and translation rights, please contact:

theculturedguides@hotmail.com

CONTENTS

History	3
Saint Mark's Square and Basilica	29
Palazzo Ducale	43
The Grand Canal	49
Churches	69

Scuola Grande di San Rocco	77
Murano	81
The Jewish Ghetto	83
The Venice Film Festival	85
Museums	89

HISTORY

If we believe tradition, Venice was founded on 25 March 421 CE. According to the *Chronicon Altinate*, on that day, three consuls sent from nearby Padua to find a suitable location for a safe commercial port chose the islet of Rialto in the Venetian lagoon, where they laid the first stone of the San Giacomo di Rialto church. Actually, the church dates to the twelfth century, which makes the whole story a bit sketchy. The *Chronicon* was an eleventh-century collection of documents and legends about the emergence of Venice and the origins of the Venetians that also included lists of popes, emperors, bishops, and doges (for over one thousand years, the *doge* was the Republic of Venice's head of state).

What we do know is that starting in the third century CE, during the Western Roman Empire's decline – culminated in 476 CE with the conquest of Ravenna, at the time the Empire's capital, by the Germanic leader Odoacer –, the inhabitants of nearby towns used to flee from the marauding barbarian hordes by taking refuge on the islands in the Venetian lagoon. They felt relatively safe there since there was hardly anything to plunder in that area, and thanks to the difficulty facing their pursuers in entering the lagoon on horseback. It was always intended as a short-term solution, though, and once the danger was over, those people returned to their homes on the mainland or what was left of them after the invaders' passage.

In the mid-fifth century, the arrival of Attila the Hun at the head of a powerful army caused more havoc than previous invasions. In 452 CE, after the fall of Aquileia, a fortified town at the eastern border of the Italian peninsula, more people than usual reached the lagoon looking to escape the nomadic invader coming from southern Siberia. This time, the situation on the mainland did not improve, which convinced the refugees to settle permanently on those islands. A long work of draining the land and securing the foundations of the first buildings began, slowly leading to the birth of a proper, if small, city.

In 466 CE, it was time for the early communities to set up a system of self-government. Their leaders met in Grado, at the Marano Lagoon's eastern tip, and agreed to have everyday matters discussed by tribunes that each of the communities would elect annually to represent them. For the next three centuries, Venetian history was heavily influenced by the events happening on the continent, such as a succession of barbarian waves in the west – mainly on the Italian peninsula – and the east, with the rise and consolidation of the Byzantine Empire. Placed on the edge of the empire, Venice enjoyed considerable autonomy, and its population and economy rapidly grew through trade, aided by its excellent shipbuilding industry.

As the city grew bigger and stronger and its wealth increased, Venice began to consider itself less an integral part of the Byzantine Empire than its ally. Over time, relationships between the proud Venetians and the emperor-appointed governors soured, not least because of differences in matters concerning the Catholic faith (the so-called iconoclast crisis was an important factor, for instance). In 742, after challenging the emperor's authority more than once, Venice's citizens finally obtained the privilege to choose their own governor – the doge – who still owed obedience to the emperor in Constantinople, at least formally.

The Republic of Venice was ruled by an oligarchy of merchants and aristocrats. Assembled in the Great Council, which acted as the city-state's legislative body, they chose a doge who ruled for life. This system of government remained almost unchanged until the last days of the Republic, in 1797.

The breaking point between Venice and its former master in the east came in 803 CE, when the doge and the other heads of the community recognized Charlemagne as emperor, thus shifting their allegiance from the Eastern Roman Emperor Nikephoros I to his Western counterpart. The Venetian Mint was founded in the mid-ninth century, and

Venice started coining its own money. A long history of incredible economic success, mainly building upon commerce, was beginning.

The ninth century was of the greatest importance in the early history of the Venetian Republic. The *Civitas Rivoalti* (the City of Rialto) was established in the middle of the lagoon on the island now home to the Sestiere of San Marco, one of six districts into which Venice is divided, called *sestieri* (meaning "a sixth part"). This is the city's most touristic neighborhood, where St. Mark's Basilica, the Doge's Palace, the La Fenice Theatre, and the Ponte dei Sospiri (the Bridge of Sighs) can be found.

Between 811 and 815 CE, a long series of talks between Franks – in the west – and Byzantines – in the east – resulted in the Treaty of Aachen (also known as Pax Nicephori, from the name of the Eastern emperor said to have taken the initiative for the negotiations), which was aimed at governing relations between the two halves of the empire, especially in the area of the Adriatic Sea. In these conditions of relative peace, the Venetian Republic could flourish despite a bitter rivalry between some of the most influential and wealthiest families.

In 828, Saint Mark the Evangelist's relic was brought to Venice, stolen from Alexandria in Egypt. St. Mark was proclaimed patron saint of the city alongside the earlier one, St. Theodore. Thus, the Winged Lion of Saint Mark became Venice's universally recognizable symbol [see drawing on page 1]. The depiction of St. Mark in the form of a lion was typical of patristic exegesis and early Christian iconography. The lion embodies the strength of the evangelist's word, while its wings suggest spiritual elevation. The lion holds a book under one of its paws – a symbol of wisdom – open on a page that reads: PAX TIBI MARCE EVANGELISTA MEVS, which means "Peace to you, Mark, my evangelist." Legend has it that Mark once was stranded on an island in the Venetian lagoon when an angel appeared to him, saying those words and signifying that the evangelist would find rest, veneration, and honor among the Venetians. And so it was.

In these first centuries of growth, the Venetians' primary economic activities were the extraction and trade of salt – as was the case for so many seaside settlements –, fishing, and the first ventures into maritime trade, primarily with the eastern part of the empire, governed from Constantinople (the ancient Byzantium, modern-day Istanbul in Turkey, the metropolis where Europe and Asia meet). In such a confined space – a group of islands in a lagoon – agricultural land was obviously scarce. To access wheat and other food, Venice was forced to quickly develop an efficient trade network, which became the foundation of its remarkable ascent in the following nine hundred years.

In a matter of a few centuries, Venice became the most important port in Europe, thanks to its unchallenged role as the gateway to the Orient. From there came the spices, the most precious fabrics, and the exquisite goods produced by a great civilization at its height. Furthermore, it was possible to establish fruitful commercial relationships with faraway India and China over Byzantium. Only much later, from the early fourteenth century, Venice started to assert its dominance over parts of northern Italy and Dalmatia, a region of Croatia overlooking the Adriatic Sea, mainly to ensure the city's safety.

The Venetians needed to protect their commercial routes in the Adriatic Sea, which led to several clashes with the Slavic peoples settled along the coast of modern-day southern Croatia who practiced piracy. In 1000 CE, Doge Pietro II Orseolo led a large fleet against those unruly populations who threatened to negatively affect Venice's rise. It is said that, on this occasion, the St. Mark's banner was hoisted on Venice's flagship, a clear sign of independence from Byzantium. The expedition was thoroughly successful, so much so that the doge returned home with the title of *Dux Dalmatiae* (commander of Dalmatia), having obtained from the Dalmatian leaders a promise of allegiance against other Slavic populaces. Lagosta, the pirates' main hub in the Adriatic Sea, was leveled.

The eleventh century was even more critical in ensuring Venice's dominance of the seas and its economic success. A masterstroke was the decision by Doge Domenico Silvo to support the Byzantine Empire in its struggle against the Normans, a northern people native of Scandinavia that had descended on Italy from Normandy, in the north of France, conquering large swaths of the peninsula's south. Led by Robert Guiscard, in 1081, the Normans invaded the Balkans, bringing the war to Constantinople's doorstep. Emperor Alexios I Komnenos, who had just ascended the throne, was wise enough to seek an alliance with Venice, hoping to take advantage of the Venetians' powerful fleet to fend off the invader.

The Venetian fleet did the job, inflicting a naval defeat on the Normans, which, however, did not prevent them from landing on the eastern Adriatic coast, getting perilously close to Constantinople. In the end, the Eastern Empire was saved by an uprising in southern Italy, which forced Robert to return and leave the enterprise's command to his son Bohemond, who proved unable to fill his father's shoes. The Venetians' help was decisive in conclusively defeating the Normans and helping the Byzantines to recapture all lost territories.

The reward for Venice's services was a source of great wealth for the city. In May 1082, Emperor Alexios issued the so-called Golden Bull. This decree granted the Venetians vast fiscal privileges throughout the Mediterranean lands of the empire. Thanks to the concessions contained in the Bull, all merchants from the erstwhile province of the empire were from now on allowed to carry on duty-free trade in many Byzantine ports of call, such as Durrës and Vlorë in modern-day Albania, Corfu, Athens, Thessaloniki, and other ports in Greece, and several ports along the coast of modern-day Turkey.

At the time, customs duties on most goods could be exorbitantly high since they were the primary source of revenue for states with no efficient internal taxation system. Considering that the Byzantine Empire was Venice's most important commercial partner by far, the Bull's effect was to give Venetian merchants a massive competitive advantage over everybody else. The city's growing prosperity was secured for centuries.

Additionally, Venice gained a foothold in the capital of the empire itself, Constantinople. There, the emperor granted the Venetians the exclusive use of a bakery, several workshops, a large warehouse, and three berths on the European side of town, a privilege unheard of. As icing on the cake, every merchant from Venice's rival Amalfi – nowadays a well-known tourist destination in southern Italy, not far from Naples – was forced to pay an annual sum of gold to the Venetian Republic if they wanted to trade with Constantinople, thus further consolidating Venice's position of supremacy in the Mediterranean Sea.

The next big step in Venice's rise involved the Holy Land. At the end of the First Crusade, launched by Pope Urban II in 1095, the Christian alliance of mostly French and Italo-Norman princes established the Kingdom of Jerusalem under the French nobleman Godfrey of Bouillon. Godfrey refused the title of king, instead choosing to be called Defender of the Holy Sepulcher. He believed only Jesus Christ could be considered the legitimate King of Jerusalem.

Only some years later, Venice could again strengthen its position in the Levant – roughly what we now call the Middle East – thanks to the aid provided to King Baldwin II of Jerusalem. In 1123, the king was taken hostage by the Artuqids, a Turkic people at the kingdom's northern border, but could escape one year later with the help of the Armenians, rivals of the Artuqids. Meanwhile, the Fatimids of Egypt had invaded the reign from the south, hoping to recapture the coastal city of Jaffa – nowadays a district on the southern fringe of Tel Aviv, in Israel – taken by the invading crusaders. Under the leadership of the French nobleman Eustace I Grenier, who ruled Jerusalem in place of the captive sovereign, the Christians defeated the Fatimids under the vizier al-Ma'mun al-Bata'ihi at the Battle of Yibneh. However, the Egyptian fleet was still a serious threat. Here came into play Venice's formidable naval force.

Doge Domenico Michiel set sail at the head of a large fleet with the aim of vanquishing the Egyptian foe also on the seas. The two fleets met off the coast of Syria, where the Venetians decisively defeated their opponents and captured several of their ships. Then, they landed in Acre, on the coast of Western Galilee. The doge went on a pilgrimage to Jerusalem, where he celebrated Christmas and met the Latin Patriarch Warmund and the Constable William I of Bures, who ruled the city in the king's absence. The three agreed that the Venetian fleet would help the crusaders storm Tyre in modern-day Lebanon or Ascalon in modern-day Israel, the only two coastal towns still in Muslim hands.

So, Venice and Jerusalem signed a treaty of alliance – the *Pactum Warmundi*, from the name of the patriarch who negotiated it – that granted *La Serenissima* (a moniker meaning "The Most Serene" that Venice earned by virtue of the remarkable stability of its political institutions) vast privileges in case of a victory over the occupiers from Egypt. After some back and forth about which target to choose first, in February 1124, the allies placed Tyre under siege, a city larger and wealthier than Ascalon that was also an important commercial hub for the hostile Damascus in Syria. A few months later, the city had fallen and the Venetians could claim their prize.

In Tyre, they were granted the possession of a large warehouse, two dozen houses, and eighteen workshops, besides a host of tax exemptions. They built a church dedicated to St. Mark (who else?) and, outside the city, were given control over several hamlets. But the Venetians' gains were much more significant than that. In every city of the kingdom, except for the capital, Jerusalem, they were allowed to possess and manage their own streets and squares, baths and markets, mills and ovens, and they could build their churches. In Acre, they obtained an entire city district, where every Venetian "may be as free as in Venice itself." In exchange for all this, Venice had to supply a contingent of armored knights to the royal army.

The Fourth Crusade was another defining moment in Venice's rise. Once again, under the pretense of religious piety, the Venetians could exploit the situation to advance their interests. Pope Innocent III, who ascended the Throne of Peter in February 1198, had immediately signaled that he wished the Christians to recapture Jerusalem, which had fallen into the hands of the Moslems after Saladin, Sultan of Egypt, had conquered it on 2 October 1187.

The French noblemen at the head of knights and crusaders decided they would land in Egypt, not Palestine, hoping to strike the enemy from the flank, where resistance would be less robust. What the crusaders lacked, though, was the significant number of ships needed to transport the troops to the other side of the Mediterranean Sea.

Thus, their commanders gathered in Venice, the only naval power capable of assembling a fleet – partly yet to be built – adequate to the task. And Doge Enrico Dandolo played his hand superbly. The Venetian fleet would transport the invasion force for free as long as the crusaders would first help the Venetians to conquer and occupy Zara (modern Zadar), a port city on the coast of modern-day Croatia on the Adriatic Sea that had rebelled against Venice's domination. Furthermore, in exchange for supplying 4,500 knights with their horses, 9,000 squires, 20,000 foot soldiers, and fifty Venetian galleys, the city was promised the payment of 85,000 silver marks – several million US dollars in today's money – in addition to half of the spoils of war. It was perhaps the best deal ever made by a doge.

Far fewer knights and foot soldiers than hoped had answered the call for the crusade, forcing the organizers to incur a large debt toward Venice just to be able to muster enough troops to complete the mission. On their part, the Venetians poured all their resources into building and arming the fleet and organizing the army to send to the Holy Land as agreed. They knew that fulfilling their part of the contract would bring honor and riches to their already prosperous city.

The Siege of Zara, in November 1202, was the first time a crusader army attacked a Christian city, which happened despite express prohibition by Pope Innocent III. It was apparent that the pope had lost control over the Fourth Crusade he was responsible for launching. The crusaders from France were up to their eyeballs in debt with the Venetians and could not afford to heed the pope's command. After two weeks of siege, the city was in the hands of the crusaders and their Venetian allies. At this point, new facts emerged that completely changed the purpose of the whole undertaking.

In Constantinople, the population was rebelling, sick and tired of having to endure the weakness of the imperial power, torn by factional struggles which caused constant instability and the frequent fall of emperors. The people were also angry at all the merchants from Venice and Genoa who had settled in the city and took advantage of the situation to bully the locals and accumulate great wealth. Doge Dandolo seized the opportunity: he convinced the crusade's commanders to divert their forces to the empire's capital and leave the liberation of the Holy Land for later.

The Venetians and Doge Dandolo harbored profound resentment at the "Greeks" for a number of perceived injustices suffered by the Venetians residing in the Eastern Empire's capital at the hands of several emperors. The doge also held a personal grudge against the city's rulers, stemming from his time as an ambassador there. He knew the

Byzantines well and was probably the only man in the expedition to have ever set foot in Constantinople. Dandolo, a very old man by then, was eager to move into action.

In April 1204, crusaders and Venetians laid siege to Constantinople, which fell after just four days. The decision by a Christian army to attack the largest Christian city in the world was unprecedented and caused widespread outrage. To add insult to injury, the invading troops did not refrain from plundering the city. Following this event, the relationship between the Catholic Church and the Orthodox Church in the east, which had always been tense since the schism in 1054, irremediably deteriorated for centuries and was only partially mended in recent times, starting in 1965 thanks to Pope Paul VI and Patriarch Athenagoras I.

The sack of Constantinople also led to the formal independence of Venice, which cut its last ties to the Byzantine Empire forever. The fall its capital city also resulted in the disintegration of the empire, with the birth of four new political entities: the Latin Empire of Constantinople, with Baldwin I, Count of Flanders and Hainaut, put on the throne by the crusaders, the Empire of Nicaea to its south, in northern Turkey, the Empire of Trebizond, on the Turkish coast overlooking the Black Sea, and the Despotate of Epirus, on Greece's western coast. Each of these small states claimed to be the legitimate heir to the erstwhile empire, which was now dissolved. The crusaders, satisfied by the riches found in Constantinople, never reached the Holy Land.

The Eastern Roman Empire could never recover and was bound to be swept away by a new, rising power: the Ottoman Empire, founded in 1299 in Anatolia, a region part of modern-day Turkey. Constantinople was conquered by the Ottoman army led by twenty-one-year-old Sultan Mehmet II on 29 May 1453 after a long siege. For the first time in its history, the city was in the hands of a Muslim ruler, where it remains to this day. The Ottoman expansion into Europe continued for another couple of centuries, leading to the conquest of the Balkans and bringing the Ottoman army to the gates of Vienna twice, in 1529 and 1683. Both times, the Turks were defeated, thus stopping the Muslim advance into European territory.

During the thirteenth and fourteenth centuries, Venice had to deal with its greatest and most dangerous rival: Genoa, on the opposite side of the Italian peninsula.

For most of the Middle Ages, commerce in the Mediterranean was dominated by the so-called maritime republics, seven Italian and one Dalmatian port cities, often at odds with each other. At the time, none of them called themselves that way. The term "maritime republics" was coined in the early nineteenth century by the Swiss historian and economist Sismondo Sismondi (1773–1842). The four main ones were Amalfi, Genoa, Pisa, and Venice, and, to this day, the flag of the Italian Navy displays their coats of arms. There were also four lesser ones: Ancona, Gaeta, Noli, and Ragusa (modern-day Dubrovnik), the only one not on Italian soil.

Each had a different historical evolution, but all shared some common threads. They were all municipal entities, i.e., self-governed city-states with their own laws and currency, accepted everywhere throughout the Mediterranean. All grew and exercised their power not by territorial expansion but through the might of their navies, capable of protecting the maritime merchant routes they used to increase their wealth and influence. All had a republican form of government, though the more powerful ones, such as Venice, gradually veered toward oligarchic rule.

Most of the eight republics succumbed to bigger neighbors sooner or later, but three – Venice, Genoa, and Ragusa – stayed independent well into the modern era. Venice, in particular, enjoyed independence from outside powers for over one thousand years! It took Napoleon's Italian campaign in 1797 to end both Genoa's and Venice's long history of self-government. At war's end, Venice came under the rule of the Archduke of Austria. At the same time, Genoa became part of the First French Empire in 1805, after a brief time as the Ligurian Democratic Republic.

In the wake of the Fourth Crusade, Venice had established its supremacy on the seas of the Levant at the expense of the Byzantine Empire. Its ancient rival Genoa, nicknamed *La Superba* ("The Haughty") by Tuscan poet, writer, and philologist Francesco Petrarca in 1358, was a commercial powerhouse in its own right. Over a period of less than two centuries, Genoa had grown from a tiny village of about 4,000 people to a naval power with settlements and emporiums reaching from Bruges in Belgium to the Crimean Peninsula – which they partially occupied – in the Black Sea. On the Atlantic coast, the Genoese kept warehouses in Lisbon and Porto in Portugal. In the Mediterranean region, they had numerous footholds on Africa's northern coast and kept several Greek and Turkish islands under their rule, besides parts of Corsica and Sardinia.

Given these premises, it had to be expected that the rivalry between Genoa and Venice would always be intense, with periods of open hostility leading to naval battles. Still, from time to time, when the circumstances demanded it, they were able to put aside their differences and make common cause against foes threatening to jeopardize the commercial interests of both cities, first and foremost the Ottomans. By 1256, though, the goodwill between the two competing republics had run out.

The first of four successive wars began after the Genoese occupied the monastery of Mar Saba (Saint Sabbas) in Acre, which at the time was the capital of the Kingdom of Jerusalem since that city had fallen under Muslim control. In the Holy Land, the relations between the Genoese and Venetian merchants had always been strained, and the Acre clashes ignited all-out warfare between the two powers. The Genoese attacked the Venetian merchant vessels docked in port and set fire to the Venetian district.

After allying with Pisa – one of the maritime republics –, Marseilles, and some French cities from the Provence region, Venice sent a powerful fleet under the command of Admiral Lorenzo Tiepolo, who would later become Venice's forty-sixth doge. The Venetian navy arrived before Acre in June 1257, broke its harbor chain, and destroyed most of the Genoese fleet. The Venetians also conquered the city's fort before agreeing to a truce with their vanquished enemies.

The Genoese, though, did not give in that easily. One year later, a large battle fleet appeared off the port of Acre. Although outnumbered, on 24 June 1258, the Venetians once again defeated the Genoese forces comprehensively, capturing twenty-five enemy galleys. In the following years, the Venetians achieved victory in another two big naval engagements, off the coasts of Greece and Sicily, respectively.

This first war, called the War of Saint Sabas after the location where hostilities began, ended only with the Peace of Cremona, signed in 1270 under the auspices of King Louis IX of France and Pope Clement IV. The pope was eager to organize the Eighth Crusade, and he needed the fleets of both sworn enemies for that enterprise. He did not live to see his dream realized: he died in November 1268 before the crusade could start.

The animosity between the two richest and most powerful maritime republics never entirely abated, and exploded anew in May 1294. At the Battle of Laiazzo, off the Turkish coast, the Venetian fleet was wiped out by the Genoese, kick-starting a new round of hostilities. After reorganizing, the Venetians sacked Genoese ports in Greece, Crimea, and Galata outside Constantinople. This led the Genoese to assault the Venetian district in the capital, where they killed most of the inhabitants. Byzantine Emperor Andronikos II Palaiologos sided with his Ligurian allies and jailed the surviving Venetians, including their chief diplomat, Marco Bembo.

In retaliation, Venice sent a battle fleet to take retribution for the emperor's betrayal. In July 1296, the Venetian vessels forced the Bosphorus Strait, sinking twenty enemy ships, destroyed the Genoese colony of Galata (nowadays a district of Istanbul), conquered Phocaea, and cast anchor before the Golden Horn right in front of the imperial palace. To prevent a full-blown war against Venice, the emperor had to pay a handsome tribute to the maritime power from Italy.

The decisive clash of the war came in September 1298, when the Venetian and Genoese fleets met before the island of Korcula in the Adriatic Sea. It was a crushing defeat for the Venetians led by Doge Andrea Dandolo, who lost eighty-four of a total of ninety-five galleys to the enemy fleet commanded by Admiral Lamba Doria. On this occasion, the Genoese captured Marco Polo, the Venetian merchant who would later become world-famous thanks to his travel memoirs known as *Il Milione*, written – or, rather, dictated – while in captivity in Genoa.

Eventually, the war-weary foes signed a peace treaty in 1299, which put an end to this phase of belligerence. Until fifty years later, when the third round of this never-ending conflict began.

In 1350, Venice allied with King Peter IV of Aragon, whose kingdom comprised most of Spain's eastern coast with its islands, Corsica, Sardinia, Sicily, and southern Italy. Peter wanted to teach the Genoese a lesson for trying to incite an insurrection against the crown in Sardinia. The powerful lagoon city was his natural ally in his endeavor.

Two naval battles marked as many tipping points in the war. First, in August 1353, the Venetian fleet under the command of Admiral Niccolò Pisani, with the help of the Aragonese navy, achieved victory against the Genoese at the Battle of Porto Conte off the western coast of Sardinia. Just over one year later, though, on 4 November 1354, the Genoese took revenge on their enemies when Admiral Pagano Doria's fleet surprised the Venetian fleet at anchor in a bay of the Greek island of Sapienza. Pisani's fleet was annihilated, leading to the loss of four or five thousand men, with another six thousand taken prisoner by the Genoese, who also could seize thirty Venetian galleys. The magnitude of this debacle was such that Venice's doge, Marino Faliero, was deposed and later beheaded for treason. In June 1355, the humiliated Venetians agreed to a peace treaty with the triumphant Republic of Genoa.

The flames of rivalry were rekindled two decades later. The Mediterranean region and surrounding area were simply too small to allow two republics with grand ambitions to coexist peacefully. In 1376, Emperor John V Palaiologos ceded the island of Tenedos to the Venetians, effectively handing them the keys to the Black Sea, where the Genoese had many interests on the Crimean Peninsula. Strategically situated at the entrance of the Dardanelles Strait, it was easy to completely block the passage between the Mediterranean and the Black Sea from there. In the hope of gaining the island for themselves, the Genoese supported a coup by John's son, who became Emperor Andronikos IV Palaiologos. But the Venetians didn't give up so easily and withstood the Genoese siege of the island in 1377.

To gain the upper hand, both powers looked for allies. Among Genoa's friends were Hungary and Austria, while Venice secured the help of the powerful Lordship of Milan, which could threaten the Ligurian city from the north. After some minor clashes, the war was decided at the southern end of the Venetian lagoon, at the port city of Chioggia. In August 1379, the Genoese conquered Chioggia, thus opening the way to the lagoon and Venice itself, which was also under attack by the Hungarians from the mainland. The situation seemed desperate until the providential intervention of the Venetian battle fleet, which had been reconstituted and descended upon Chioggia in January 1380, led by eighty-year-old Doge Andrea Contarini and Admiral Vettor Pisani.

The Genoese fleet was now trapped, and the besiegers had become besieged. In June of that same year, they had to surrender. The war ended with the Peace of Turin, signed in August 1381 between all participants. Venice was safe but at a high price. It was forced to relinquish control over Dalmatia to the King of Hungary and Treviso to the Duke of Austria.

The island of Tenedos went to the House of Savoy. Financially, this last war had been disastrous for Venice, but Genoa was even worse off and never recovered.

* * *

Messer (Mister) Marco Polo came from a wealthy merchant family like so many others in Venice at the time. His father, Niccolò, and his two uncles, Marco and Matteo, managed a thriving commercial enterprise with branch offices in Constantinople, Sudak (Crimea), and probably some other port cities in the Levant open to Venetian traders. They were used to traveling long and dangerous routes into Asia, reaching as far as Persia (modern-day Iran) and even China. Once, Niccolò and Matteo stayed in Bukhara, in modern-day Uzbekistan, for three years straight, giving them a knowledge of that region few, if any, of their peers could claim.

When they came back from their latest travel in 1269, after an extended stay at the court of Kublai Khan, Great Khan of the Mongols and Emperor of China, they brought back gifts for the Catholic Pope with the request for teachers with a solid grounding in the liberal arts, to send to China to educate the emperor's court about the Christian religion. After obtaining letters from Pope Gregory X and presents for the Great Khan, Niccolò and Matteo set out again, taking Marco with them. It was 1271, and the young heir was only 17.

The result of an incredibly far and long-lasting expedition that took the three Polos twenty-four years to complete was that masterpiece of travel writing known as *Il Milione* (*The Travels of Marco Polo*), which Marco dictated to his fellow prisoner Rustichello da Pisa when the two were held in the San Giorgio prison in Genoa after the Battle of Korcula, in 1298. Marco Polo, a merchant and traveler, had in mind a book that would serve as a merchant's manual to be used by traders as a guide for their long-distance trips into Asia. Rustichello, on the other hand, being a novelist, conceived more of a novel than an essay and transformed his companion Marco into something like a hero in search of adventure.

It is also possible that the initial idea developed by the two men in captivity was that of a geographical treatise as vast as possible and that only later the famous descriptions of fantastical places and facts were added to that original merchants' guide. However, the fascination the book has exercised over the centuries on generations of readers largely depends on the beauty and appeal of precisely those legends and embellished tales. This book's influence on its time cannot be denied if even personalities like Portugal's Prince Henry the Navigator and famed seaman and explorer Christopher Columbus owned a copy.

At times, Marco Polo's profession and the intent of his trip come out, such as with the detailed descriptions of freighters – including the number of masts, the shape and surface area of their sails, their ability to weather stormy seas – or the listing of prices of goods and merchandise, often comparing them with prices found in Europe. The book's central part is almost entirely dedicated to the time – seventeen years – spent by the Polos at the court and in the service of the Great Khan in the capital Dadu (or Khanbaliq, "the Khan's city"), modern-day Peking, and embarking on several missions throughout the empire on his behest.

In the end, in 1292, the Khan reluctantly allowed the three Venetians to join a naval expedition leaving China bound for Persia, accompanying a Chinese princess. After an eighteen-month navigation, punctuated by several shore stops, they finally landed at Hormuz, in modern-day Iran, and from there continued their travel on land, touching Tabriz (in northwestern Iran), Trebizond (on the northern Turkish coast), and Constantinople, before getting home. They reached Venice in 1295, almost twenty-five years after leaving. All three men were still alive, which was a minor miracle in and by itself.

* * *

After its latest clash with Genoa on the seas and in the lagoon and the resultant Peace of Turin, Venice pursued a more forceful penetration strategy into its own hinterland. Territorial expansion in the Po valley, which pitted Venice against Milan, and the defense of its eastern dominions against the Turks were the dominant motifs of Venice's foreign policy for over a century. In a period that went from 1389 to 1509, *La Serenissima* conquered and subjugated a long list of independent cities and duchies, beginning with Treviso nearby and never stopping until most of Italy's northeast was in its hands. In 1509, Venice's *Stato da Tera* – its mainland possessions – reached its maximum expansion.

As so often happens to empires and powerful nations, Venice entered a phase of decline at the apex of its ascent that would last almost three centuries. It ended in 1797 with the defeat against Napoleon and the temporary annexation to Austria. Two events beyond its control ushered in Venice's long downfall into irrelevance.

First, in 1453, Constantinople was captured by the advancing Turks. The Ottoman Empire was quickly expanding along routes that were central to Venice's commercial interests, causing the lagoon city to lose all the privileges it had secured from the former Christian rulers and cutting its merchants out from access to all those high-prized goods coming from India and China that were at the heart of its wealth, namely pepper, nutmeg, cloves, cinnamon, ginger, as well as silk, porcelain, dyes, and noble woods. Muslim merchants were now the unescapable middlemen who enriched themselves in those lucrative trades.

Then, in 1492, the Genoese explorer Christopher Columbus "discovered" America on a mission by the Spanish crown, landing at the island of San Salvador in the Bahamas. Slowly but surely, the world was getting bigger and bigger; new trading routes were opened over the oceans, and the importance of the Mediterranean started dwindling. Countries like Spain, Portugal, and the Netherlands gained importance at the expense of the Italian maritime republics. By the end of the sixteenth century, the British Empire was beginning to take shape, eventually comprising territories and commercial hubs scattered all over the globe, such as Canada, parts of the Caribbean, Africa from the northern coast up to the Cape of Good Hope at its southern tip, India, and Australia.

To make matters even worse, between 1630 and 1631, the Great Plague killed up to one-third of Venice's population, leaving behind misery and despair. When, on 12 May 1797, Napoleon subjugated the Republic of Venice and deposed its last doge, Ludovico Manin, the erstwhile superpower was but a shadow of its former self. After a time under the Austrians, Venice and the Veneto region became part of the newborn Kingdom of Italy through a plebiscite in October 1866.

SAINT MARK'S SQUARE AND BASILICA

By far the most famous and most visited Venetian public square, Piazza San Marco is home to the Basilica by the same name and just steps from Venice's most prominent noble palace, the magnificent Palazzo Ducale. Saint Mark's Square can be considered Venice's only actual square. Indeed, all other plazas of the lagoon city are called either *campo* or *campiello* ("small field"). The only other square worthy of the name is Piazzale Roma, near Venice's Santa Lucia rail station, the furthest cars and buses coming from the mainland can progress when entering the city. From there, visitors can reach any part of Venice by *vaporetto*, the city's omnipresent waterbuses.

Originally, the area now covered by the square was a garden crossed by the rio (brook) Batario. With the arrival of St. Mark's remains in 828, the construction of the first basilica began, greatly increasing the importance of this part of town in ancient Venice's urban plan. In 1156, Doge Vitale II Michiel had the Batario drained and filled in. That allowed several more buildings to rise in the square, which slowly became the monumental heart of the city. Already in 1063, under Doge Domenico I Contarini, the construction of the current basilica had started. In 1264, Doge Renier Zen commissioned the square's beautiful pavement in herringbone bricks.

Piazza San Marco is widely considered one of the most stunning squares in the world, to the extent that Napoleon Bonaparte, Emperor of the French, went so far as to hail it as "the most beautiful hall in Europe." It is also the lowest patch of land in the whole city and, therefore, the first to get flooded by the infamous *acqua alta* – the high water that has always tormented Venice's inhabitants. When that happens, elevated walkways are installed to allow for the transit of pedestrians. October, November, and December are the months during which this phenomenon is more common, even though, due to the rise in the level of the Adriatic Sea, high waters are increasingly frequent also in Spring.

Today, the trapezoid-shaped square covers an area of about 138,000 square feet, being almost 600 feet long and 230 feet wide on average. It is closed by the iconic St. Mark's Basilica on its eastern side and by three imposing buildings known as *Procuratiae* on the other three sides. The Procuratiae get their name from the purpose they were employed for: Venice's high government officials and prosecutors – the procurators – had their offices there. The building on the northern side of the square, on the left looking toward the basilica, is the Procuratie Vecchie (the old Procuratie); the one opposite to it, on the square's southern side, is the Procuratie Nuove (the new Procuratie); the one closing the square at its western side, opposite the basilica, is called Procuratie Nuovissime (the newest Procuratie), or Ala Napoleonica (the Napoleonic Wing).

Their names give away the order in which those edifices were built. The oldest starts at the magnificent Clock Tower and is 498 feet long. It has a portico of no less than fifty arches, to which correspond one hundred windows on the two higher floors. This one was built between 1517 and 1538 under three different doges. The Procuratie Nuove, constructed between 1583 and 1640, extends all the way to the world-famous Campanile di San Marco, the square's bell tower. It served as a Royal Palace at the time of the Italic Kingdom concocted by Napoleon – that survived from 1805 to 1814 – and kept that function under the Savoy, from 1866 to 1946. Today, it hosts several museums and a part of the Marciana National Library, the city's largest and most important. The Napoleonic Wing, as the name suggests, was built on the orders of the conquering emperor, who, to this end, tore down the church of San Geminiano, dating back to the sixteenth century and done in Renaissance style. It is now home to part of the Correr Museum.

Apart from St. Mark's Basilica [see cover image], the square's highlights are the Clock Tower at its northeast corner and the St. Mark's Bell Tower opposite it. The Clock Tower is a Renaissance tower, built between 1496 and 1499 – the central body – but expanded and renovated in 1506 and 1757. When the tower was inaugurated, its clock was one of only three clocks with mechanical movements worldwide. It is an engineering marvel, featuring a Virgin and Child in gilt metal sitting on a throne and flanked by two doors used for the procession of the Magi. On only two days of the year, on the Feast of the Epiphany and Ascension Day, the door on Mary's left opens every hour on the hour. Four figures appear in a semicircle before the Virgin: the angel who announces the birth of Jesus, followed by the Three Wise Men. They all curtsey the Virgin Mary, and the angel raises the trumpet to play it while the Magi lift their crowns and present gifts to the Child. They all reenter from the door at the right of the Virgin.

Another spectacular device is a couple of bronze statues at the tower's very top. Venetians call them *I Do' Mori* (the two Moors) because of their dark color. The statues depict two shepherds who strike the hours on a large bronze bell with their mallets. The Moors, about eight feet tall, were cast in 1497. They have bodies divided in half at waist height, allowing the torso to rotate to strike the bell surmounted by a golden globe and a cross. The bell was also cast that same year and is five feet tall.

Together, the whole sculptural group weighs in at twenty-five tons.

The two Moors are pretty similar, but the one on the left is bearded, whereas the one on the right is not. That's because they play two different roles: the bearded one, nicknamed "the old," marks the hours two minutes early to signify the time already passed. Conversely, the other one, nicknamed "the young," marks the hours two minutes late to indicate the time to come.

One more unique feature of this landmark is the space dedicated to St. Mark's Lion, just below the bell. Standing before a blue, starred background, it is apparent how the statue is moved to the left in its niche. The reason is simple: to the lion's right stood the statue of Doge Agostino Barbarigo, who had inaugurated the tower in 1499. After the French occupied Venice in 1797, the doge's statue and those of many other doges found throughout the city were destroyed.

The last architectural detail worth mentioning is the tower's deliberate symbolism. At the very top of man's life stands time, whose passing no one can escape. Just below, the Lion of Venice symbolizes the power of the Republic, which exceeds that of the Church, set just beneath it in the form of the Virgin seated on a throne. It is arguable that the clock, one level lower and decorated with zodiac signs, symbolizes scientific knowledge.

The San Marco Bell Tower is one of Venice's most recognizable symbols, and for good reason. It is both lovely and impressive, as well as having a fascinating history. It is nicknamed by Venice's citizens *El paron de casa* (the lord of the house) since it welcomes visitors to the city, telling them the history of the Serenissima and giving them the most stunning views from its belfry 180 feet in the sky. On clear days, it is possible to see the Dolomites mountain range in the distance. No other than Galileo Galilei – the universally famous physicist, mathematician, astronomer, and one of the fathers of modern science – once took advantage of its considerable height to demonstrate his telescope in 1609.

The tower's construction began in the late ninth century under Doge Pietro Tribuno. Conceived initially as a watchtower and lighthouse, it underwent numerous restorations over the centuries to repair damage caused by lightning, fires, and earthquakes. At 323 feet in total height, it is Venice's tallest building to this day and one of the tallest bell towers in Italy.

The tower is made in late-medieval Romanesque style. The main body has a square plan with a side of approximately 40 feet and a height of almost 170 feet. On top of that is a beautiful, white belfry on which rests the bell tower brick attic. It features high-relief sculptures on its four sides, two each of the Lion of Saint Mark and a symbolic figure of Venice as Justice. Everything is crowned by a spire made of wood, destroyed multiple times by fires caused by human recklessness or lightning. On top of the spire, a gilded wooden statue of the archangel Gabriel acts as a weathervane, bringing the total height of this magnificent landmark to 323 feet. The current statue dates to 1822 and is the work of Italian sculptor Luigi Zandomeneghi.

Its eastern side, facing the Basilica and Palazzo Ducale, is graced with a loggia called Loggetta del Sansovino from the name of its creator, the Italian architect and sculptor Jacopo Tatti, known as "il Sansovino." It was built between 1537 and 1549 as a triumphal arch where Venice's noblemen could assemble before or after acceding to one of the government buildings of Piazza San Marco. The façade features three arches framed by four columns, in whose niches stand the bronze statues of Minerva, Mercury, Apollo, and Peace, all by Sansovino.

Today's Campanile (bell tower) is just over one hundred years old, having been completely rebuilt after the tower collapsed in 1902, leaving only a pile of rubber. For months, the structure had shown signs of weakening, in the shape of cracks getting bigger and bigger, threatening the stability of the construction. Thanks to the previous worrying signs of fragility, when the tower came down on the morning of 14 July 1902, nobody was hurt because the area had already been cleared of people. Thankfully, it was immediately decided to rebuild the Campanile precisely as it was before its collapse, retaining the architecture and materials resulting from centuries of interventions up to the sixteenth century, when the tower got its final appearance. As Mayor Filippo Grimani famously proclaimed on 25 Aprile 1903, laying the first stone, the tower would be rebuilt "as it was, where it was." Nine years later, the new Bell Tower in its ancient form was again inaugurated.

Consuming food and drinks, as well as feeding the omnipresent pigeons, is not allowed in the whole square. And watch out for seagulls: they can sometimes get aggressive with people, especially if you carry food. Venice is one of the most popular tourist destinations in the world, which, together with a lot of money, also brings overcrowding and occasional inconveniences. In the last years, the city administration introduced a series of ordinances to get some order to the unending onslaught of tourists without killing the golden goose. If you want to enjoy your meal outdoors, you can stop – from Wednesday to Sunday – in the Royal Gardens overlooking the Grand Canal, a few steps away.

* * *

The Basilica di San Marco (St. Mark's Basilica) is one of Venice's most recognizable landmarks, together with the famous Bell Tower and Palazzo Ducale nearby. It is the cathedral of the Diocese of Venice and the seat of the patriarchate. The title of *patriarch* is the highest title a Christian bishop can have; in Europe, only the Bishop of Lisbon (Portugal) and the Bishop of Venice currently hold the title. In his role as Bishop of Rome, the pope traditionally was named Patriarch of the West before Pope Benedict XVI abolished that title in 2006.

The original basilica was built between 828 and 832 CE to house the relics of St. Mark, smuggled out of Alexandria (Egypt) to make him the protector of the city, and was supposed to be an extension of the adjacent Doge's Palace – the old one, built under Doge Pietro IV Candiano toward the end of the tenth century. Building a basilica was necessary to establish Venice as an independent episcopal see. This first church was meant to replace the pre-existing palace chapel. The church was soon considered Venice's monument par excellence, and public and religious life gravitated around it. All the city's most important anniversaries were celebrated here, and the election of every doge, the supreme magistrate of the Republic, was officially sanctioned here.

In 1063, Doge Domenico I Contarini commissioned a new basilica, extravagant enough to symbolize Venice's power and wealth before the world. Following the model of the Basilica of the Holy Apostles in Constantinople, that city's second most important church, San Marco features a Greek cross plan, five large domes, and an enticing blend of Ancient and Oriental art. The well-known Victorian-era British painter, writer, and art critic John Ruskin described the basilica in the second volume of *The Stones of Venice*:

" [...] there rises a vision out of the earth, and all the great square seems to have opened from it in a kind of awe, that we may see it far away;—a multitude of pillars and white domes, clustered into a long low pyramid of colored light; a treasure-heap, it seems, partly of gold, and partly of opal and mother-of-pearl, hollowed beneath into five great vaulted porches, ceiled with fair mosaic, and beset with sculpture of alabaster, clear as amber and delicate as ivory,—sculpture fantastic and involved, of palm leaves and lilies, and grapes and pomegranates, and birds clinging and fluttering among the branches, all twined together into an endless network of buds and plumes; and in the midst of it, the solemn forms of angels, sceptered, and robed to the feet, and leaning to each other across the gates, their figures indistinct among the gleaming of the golden ground through."

A few meters before the Basilica's entrance stand three bronze flag poles with bases decorated by Venetian sculptor Alessandro Leopardi, erected in 1505 to replace three older and simpler ones. Their low reliefs have precise meanings. On the center one, Leopardi sculpted Justice and an elephant, which represents strength and prudence – the hallmarks of good governance. The pole base on the right, nearer to the water, depicts Nereids and Tritons – mythological sea creatures – carrying the fruits of the sea. On the left, nearer to the land, a satyr – a minor deity representing the life force of nature – offers a vine to Triton, son of Poseidon, Ancient Greece's sea god.

The three beautiful red poles, each with a golden Lion of St. Mark at the top, are named after Cyprus, Crete, and Morea (the Peloponnese), to mean the three reigns conquered by the Venetians. In the past, the flag poles sported the banners of those three kingdoms. That is no longer the case, of course, and nowadays, the flags of Venice, Italy, and the European Union are sometimes flown from them.

The Basilica was inaugurated in 1094 under

Doge Vitale Falier and, over time, underwent several refurbishments that gave it its current appearance. At a time when most of Europe was experimenting with the aesthetics and structural feasibility of Romanesque architecture, the Basilica was deliberately built in Byzantine style, also calling Greek architects to contribute with their ideas. The church was made ever more sumptuous year after year, both inside and outside, until the rulers of Venice were satisfied with its unrivaled grandeur. The façade, for instance, was completely rebuilt between the thirteenth and fourteenth centuries, covering it in marble and adding several arches to it, and the five domes were raised. By 1607, when the two last altars were placed inside, the Basilica could be considered complete, now a fascinating combination of successive architectural styles.

The building is 250 feet long and 205 feet wide at the transept, with the main dome 141 feet tall. Comparing it with other famous cathedrals around Europe, it is noticeable how the laguna's sandy ground compelled its designers to build in width much more than in height to better distribute its weight. The bronze doors are from different eras; the central one dates to the twelfth century, while the one on the right (southern) end – Porta di San Clemente – is the oldest, dating back to the eleventh century. The minor doors are more recent.

The basilica has a Greek cross plan with four arms divided into three naves. The central naves are covered by five domes, the lateral ones by a barrel-vaulted ceiling. A narthex – a small space serving as a vestibule that separates the façade from the naves – divided into small domed bays precedes the church's interior on three sides of the front arm. It is opened by five arches decorated with medieval low reliefs of extraordinary beauty. This atrium visually prepares the visitor for the overwhelming splendor that explodes in an incredible triumph of gold and colors inside the church.

This remarkable space, so richly decorated with columns and pillars, whose floor is done in precious multicolored marble, appears almost weightless. The countless mosaics – over 40,000 square feet – on a gold background, which cover walls, vaults, and domes, expand the space, concealing the massive wall structure and the mighty pillars thanks to the play of colors originating in their golden and blue reflections. Of all the mosaics on the façade, the only surviving original one is the one surmounting the first door on the left, the Porta di Sant'Alipio, which depicts the scene of St. Mark's body being moved to the ancient basilica. Due to the damage taken over the centuries, all the others had to be redone – maintaining the original subjects – between the seventeenth and nineteenth centuries.

One of the most exciting pieces at the Basilica is the quadriga in gilded and silver-plated bronze that dominates the church's main entrance, the Horses of San Marco. It was looted by the Venetians from the Hippodrome of Constantinople during the victorious Fourth Crusade and displayed on Venice's most revered landmark as a show of strength. It is also the only original sculptural group of its kind left in the world. Actually, the statues on display in the open are a copy. The original ones were painstakingly restored at the end of the 1970s and are now exhibited inside the Basilica Museum.

PALAZZO DUCALE

Palazzo Ducale – the Doge's Palace – has always been the main symbol of the Republic's institutional traditions, independence, and mercantile power, with the resulting riches. Although its official address is Piazza San Marco, 1 – or simply San Marco, 1 – its western façade faces a slightly smaller square called Piazzetta San Marco, while its southern and eastern sides overlook the San Marco Basin and the Rio di Palazzo – a smaller canal – respectively. Its northern side adjoins the Basilica, which closes its inner courtyard.

The first Palace of the Doge was located on the mainland in Heraclia (today's Eraclea). That's where the first doge, Paolo Lucio Anafesto, resided, around 700-717 CE. The doge's seat was moved a couple of times in the following decades until, in 812, Doge Agnello Partecipazio decided to settle in Rivoaltus – today's Rialto – where he built his new palace on a plot of land he owned. In the guise of a stout castle, this building rose on the site now occupied by the current palace. It was completed around 970 under Doge Pietro IV Candiano. It had to be an opulent dwelling if even Emperor Otto III, who visited Venice in 998, was impressed by the luxury of the interior spaces.

Between 1173 and 1177, on orders by Doge Sebastiano Ziani, the whole area of San Marco underwent a major reorganization, including renovation and extension works of the palace. Another emperor, Frederick Barbarossa, was a guest at the palace for a remarkable two months after signing a peace treaty with Pope Alexander III in 1177 – the Peace of Venice – brought about by the emperor's defeat against the Lombard League at the Battle of Legnano one year earlier. Between 1301 and 1581, restructuring of the Doge's Palace rarely stopped, be it to reorganize the interior spaces in the wake of a growing Great Council – the Republic's highest political body – or to repair damages caused by big fires (at least three between 1483 and 1577).

A masterpiece of Gothic art, the Doge's Palace is the pre-eminent example of Venetian-Byzantine architecture in town, perfectly illustrating the deep relationship linking La Serenissima to the Eastern Roman Empire, both in cultural and commercial terms. As a testament to architects and sculptors who worked on it over centuries, the palace's imposing structure succeeds in creating the impression of lightness, thanks to a long, two-tiered colonnade made of finely inlaid columns rich in decorative elements reminiscent of lace. As is a necessity in

Venice, the whole construction rests on a raft of larch trunks that supports a basement made of Istrian stone – a compact limestone rock similar to marble much used in the area.

The palace consists of three main buildings. The oldest wing is the one facing the San Marco Basin. The Sala del Gran Consiglio – the Hall of the Great Council – is housed here, the largest room in the palace, where Venice's noblemen congregated to elect the doge and make the most consequential decisions, such as initiating a war. Foreign dignitaries were brought to this hall to admire the Republic's most significant military victories, depicted on the many paintings hanging from its walls. Most of what is visible dates to after 1577, when a catastrophic fire almost destroyed the palace. The Hall of the Great Council is 172 feet in length and 80 feet in width, thus covering a surface area of nearly 14,000 square feet. Its ceiling is a remarkable 37½ feet high.

The wing facing Piazzetta San Marco was built starting in 1424 under Doge Francesco Foscari and replaced the old palace-fortress. Its façade was modeled after the one overlooking the San Marco Basin, which is evident at first glance. Both are done in Gothic-Venetian style, with an elaborate upper volume defined by inlaid marbles and a series of large ogival windows, with one central, grand balcony each. This wing served as the city's courthouse. In its magnificent Sala dello Scrutinio (Scrutiny Room), formerly the palace's Library, the votes concerning all political elections in the Venetian Republic were counted and certified, including the most important one when the new doge was elected.

The southern façade, overlooking the water, is 234 feet wide, with seventeen arches making up its ground floor. The western façade, overlooking the square, has one additional arch, thus reaching a length of 245 feet. Among the many architectural details making this palace an unmissable attraction, three statues on the colonnade's second level deserve a special mention: a trio of archangels, each with its meaning and symbolism. In the northwest corner of the palace, Gabriel symbolizes government and justice; in the southwest corner, Michael, armed with his traditional sword, represents war and victory over evil; in the southeast corner, Raphael stands for trade and God's protection.

The eastern block is the most recent one, built after the 1483 fire in Renaissance style and completed in 1560. The doge's apartments and several government offices were housed in this wing, which is much less richly decorated than the palace's two main ones. On the opposite side of the Rio di Palazzo lies the building called Prigioni Nove, the New Prisons, connected to the Doge's Palace by the famous Ponte dei Sospiri, Venice's Bridge of Sighs.

A little artistic jewel not to be missed is the so-called Porta della Carta (Card Door), the monumental entrance to the Doge's Palace sandwiched between the Palace and the Basilica. Built between 1439 and 1442 under Doge Francesco Foscari, its sculptural apparatus was originally painted and gold-plated. Its name probably derives from the presence nearby of a scribe with his desk, who was available to write letters and contracts for the many illiterates who were part of every city's populace before the introduction of compulsory education.

The iconography of this portal of stunning beauty is dedicated to the subject of justice since this is the part of the Palace where offenders were brought to be judged after entering from this door. At the very top, the statue of Justice, holding a sword and scales, leaves no doubt as to who is the master here. Just below it, a bust of Mark the Evangelist dominates the large, elaborate stained glass window. At the bottom of the window, there's a figure of Doge Foscari, the portal's patron, kneeling in front of Venice's Winged Lion in sign of deference. The other four statues on both sides of the entrance stand for the cardinal virtues essential to good governance: Justice and Prudence on the sides of St. Mark's Lion, Fortitude and Temperance beneath them.

Nowadays, Palazzo Ducale is one of the city's foremost museums and the third most visited museum in Italy. Inside, visitors are guided through many rooms, including spectacular institutional rooms, the doge's apartments, and the armory. The visit also includes the prison, across the Rio di Palazzo via the Bridge of Sighs, whose name derives from the sighs prisoners were said to breathe when they saw the light of day, possibly for the last time. Many works by such renowned Venetian painters as Jacopo and Domenico Tintoretto, Titian, Francesco Bassano, and many others grace the walls and ceilings inside the palace.

Two massive columns made of marble and granite welcome visitors arriving by boat from the lagoon at the entrance of Piazzetta San Marco. They came from Constantinople, brought to Venice as spoils of war, and erected under Doge Sebastiano Zani, who ruled the Republic from 1172 to 1178. Apparently, a third column was lost in the basin mud and never recovered. The trunk of both columns is about 40 feet tall, to which a 3-foot capital is added. On top of the column on the left accessing the square stands a statue of Saint Theodore slaying a dragon. Theodore, whom the Venetians call Todaro, was the city's first patron saint before being replaced by Saint Mark. The column on the right features a statue of the ubiquitous Winged Lion of St. Mark, which is, in fact, an ancient sculpture of a lion coming from Greece or Syria, to which a pair of wings was later added.

THE GRAND CANAL

No visit to Venice would be complete without a tour of the Grand Canal, Venice's main waterway, which divides the city's historic center into two parts. Either by taking a romantic gondola tour or by simply navigating the canal aboard a vaporetto, visitors are afforded the easiest and most efficient way of getting to appreciate the beauty and opulence of many of Venice's most prominent aristocratic mansions, not to mention its four bridges, each with its own personality. The canal, akin to a giant winding snake paving its way in the city's very heart, is 2.4 miles long and measures between 100 and 230 feet in width, with an average depth of 18 feet.

The Piazzale Roma stop of the 1 line is where visitors arriving by car or bus would start their journey, at the northernmost stop of any waterbus navigating the canal. On their way to San Marco, they will pass many of Venice's most interesting sights, some of which merit a more direct visit, by disembarking and continuing the trip on board of a later boat. From north to south, here is a selection of landmarks worth mentioning.

BRIDGES

There are precisely four bridges crossing the canal. Southbound from the terminal at Piazzale Roma, the first bridge one encounters is also the canal's most modern one.

<u>Ponte della Costituzione</u> (Constitution Bridge)

Better known by Venetians as Ponte di Calatrava, from the name of the Spanish – naturalized Swiss – star architect and engineer Santiago Calatrava who designed it, this bridge was only opened to the public in 2008 and has since been mired in controversy. It is a vital pedestrian crossing, considering it connects Piazzale Roma to Venice's central train station, Santa Lucia, across the canal. Mainly made using steel, glass, and Istrian stone, it is very different from the other bridges on the Grand Canal.

The famous architect's guiding idea was a visual challenge to gravity, expressed through curved lines, conveying a sense of lightness and transparency. The bridge's lower support structure is inspired by a fish spine. Seventy-four steel ribs form the structure's backbone, while five arches carry its weight and stabilize it. Initially, it was planned for the construction works to last fifteen months, but in the end, it took almost six years to see the bridge completed. Its name was proposed by philosophy professor Massimo Cacciari, then-mayor of Venice, to honor the Italian Republican Constitution on the sixtieth anniversary of its promulgation.

Much went wrong during construction and afterward. Construction costs soared from the envisioned 6.7 million euros to 11.3 million, not including the small cable car that had to be added after completion when it became apparent that the bridge was inaccessible for people with disabilities or elders. The bridge floor, built of glass panes, was much too slippery even for perfectly able pedestrians, especially when wet from rain. To add insult to injury, the semi-transparent motorized cabin installed on one side of the bridge at a cost of a further 1.8 million never entered service. It was dismantled in May 2020 without ever having carried a passenger. Repair and maintenance costs are the highest of any bridge in Venice due to the need to replace many glass panes every year.

Despite its well-publicized shortcomings, the Calatrava Bridge, which Venetians wryly renamed "Bridge of the Fallen" due to its many victims, remains a beautiful sight from both sides of the canal and a useful shortcut between the two main points of arrival for all visitors coming from the mainland.

Ponte degli Scalzi (Bridge of the "barefoot monks")

This stone bridge is not far from the Calatrava Bridge and connects another end of the Santa Lucia landing with the heart of old Venice. Due to its proximity to the train station, Venetians also call it the Station Bridge. Its real name derives from the church located on the northern end of the bridge, Santa Maria di Nazareth (Saint Mary of Nazareth), or Chiesa degli Scalzi, an eighteenth-century church that was the seat of the Carmelitani Scalzi – the Discalced Carmelites – monastic order in town.

This beautiful, single-vault bridge was built between May 1932 and October 1934 – under Fascist rule – to replace the preexistent one, which was an ugly, rectilinear, cast-iron bridge erected in 1858, when Venice was part of the Austro-Hungarian Empire. Entirely made of the traditional Istrian stone, it was built without the help of reinforced concrete or iron parts. Its parapet is hollow and conceals the necessary piping. From the top of the bridge, visitors can enjoy a spectacular view over the northern segment of the Grand Canal.

Ponte di Rialto (Rialto Bridge)

The Rialto Bridge is Venice's best-known among tourists and visitors to the city. It is also the oldest of today's bridges on the Grand Canal. It was inaugurated in 1591 after three years of work on a project by Venetian architect Antonio da Ponte and replaced a thirteenth-century wooden bridge in the same spot that had collapsed twice already under the weight of pedestrians, besides catching fire more than once.

To connect the two banks of the Grand Canal near the Rialto market, which was the city's most important, a pontoon bridge had been built in 1181. It was replaced by a more solid and permanent wooden structure supported by piles around 1250, which collapsed in 1444 under the weight of thousands of onlookers gathered to take a glimpse at the wedding procession of the Marquis of Ferrara Leonello d'Este of the mighty Este dynasty – lords of Ferrara, Modena, and Reggio –, who was marrying as his second wife Maria of Aragon, an illegitimate child of King Alfonso V of Aragon – also sovereign of Naples, Sardinia, Sicily, and Jerusalem.

The wooden bridge was then rebuilt a little wider and with a movable part to allow for the passage of masted boats. Serving as an access to the Rivoalto (now Rialto) market more than anything else, it took its name. On the bridge itself, a host of shops and commercial activities established themselves, whose rent went into Venice's state coffers, thus helping pay for the bridge's maintenance and upkeep.

When, in 1554, the Republic launched a tender to design a stone bridge to be built in place of the old wooden one, which was getting inadequate to satisfy the public's necessities and too expensive to maintain, the most celebrated architects of the time were invited to participate – names such as Michelangelo, Andrea Palladio, and Jacopo Sansovino, truly the best of the best. After much discussion and controversy, all projects by the biggest stars of the era were discarded in favor of one by the humbler architect and engineer Antonio da Ponte, which allowed easy transit in the Grand Canal to the large barges transporting goods to the nearby market and the adjacent storehouses.

Due to dramatic events like a terrible plague between 1575 and 1577 and the big fire of the Doge's Palace in 1577, construction work did not begin until 1588, under Doge Pasquale Cicogna. More than twelve thousand elm wood poles were used to support the structure's foundation, and the final cost of this iconic landmark reached the staggering sum of 250,000 Venetian ducats. In one of his famous landscapes, celebrated Venetian artist Canaletto once painted the bridge as designed (and never realized) by Palladio.

Ponte dell'Accademia (Academy Bridge)

The Grand Canal's southernmost bridge is hardly the most beautiful in the lagoon city. Still, it has a fascinating history and is noteworthy for connecting the San Marco district to a neighborhood – the Dorsoduro district – with two of Venice's foremost museums: the Accademia Galleries and the Peggy Guggenheim Collection. It was the main public project carried out during the third and last period of Austrian rule, between 1848 and 1866, before Venice became part of the newly formed Kingdom of Italy.

On 20 November 1854, the Ponte della Carità – Charity Bridge, taking its name from the nearby Carità complex, which included a convent, a school building, and the church of Santa Maria della Carità, buildings now housing the Accademia Galleries – opened to the public as a pedestrian toll bridge. It was built of steel and wood but soon showed worrisome signs of corrosion and deterioration, which convinced the Fascist administration to replace it with a temporary substitute while waiting to construct a final stone bridge, more worthy of the city's importance.

Italian engineer Eugenio Miozzi, who was already working on the Ponte della Libertà (originally Ponte Littorio), the 2.4 miles-long road bridge connecting Venice to the mainland, completed a wooden structure in just thirty-seven days. The bridge was effectively finished on 15 January 1933 but was only inaugurated on 19 February after installing a gas line along the bridge's arch. Due in part to the outbreak of World War II and the costs associated with building a brand-new stone bridge, the "temporary" label was soon forgotten. The Ponte dell'Accademia has become a staple of the Grand Canal's landscape. So much so that the inhabitants of Venice jokingly coined the expression "as temporary as the Accademia Bridge."

MANSIONS

Many of Venice's most spectacular and historically significant mansions overlook the Grand Canal. They are done in four main architectural styles: Venetian-Byzantine, up to the thirteenth century; Gothic, in the fourteenth and fifteenth centuries; Renaissance, from the mid-fifteenth century to the end of the sixteenth century; and Baroque, which defined the seventeenth and eighteenth centuries with ever more grandiose and extravagant palaces.

Fontego dei Turchi (Fondaco of the Turks)

Coming from the north, the first prominent Grand Canal palace is this majestic building on the waterway's right side. *Fontego* is the Venetian word for the Italian *fondaco*, which stands for a warehouse intended for the goods of foreign merchants in town, hence the name. The Fontego dei Turchi was built as a sizeable patrician residence around the half of the thirteenth century by Giacomo Palmieri, progenitor of the noble Pesaro family, who was the consul of the municipality of Pesaro in Venice.

Over the centuries, it changed hands many times, its ownership mainly depending on Venice's commercial and political interests and alliances. For a time, it was awarded to the Marquis of Ferrara as a sign of gratitude for his help in one of the Republic's wars against Genoa. This beautiful and imposing residence had its own dock, a staircase adorning its façade, a courtyard equipped with wells and benches, mezzanines, and servants' quarters. The interior was richly decorated, sporting small fountains, marble columns and stairs, as well as vases made of gold and silver.

In 1621, the mansion was finally assigned to the Turkish merchants in town, who held it for a couple of centuries. The building underwent major works in this phase to better suit its new role. The Serenissima demolished the two side turrets to remove a symbol of nobility and deprive the foreigners of a chance to spy on the city. While the sleeping quarters were housed on the three upper floors, the ground floor was a warehouse. It also had a large room serving as a mosque and some space reserved for the Turks' ritual bath. Inside, European Muslims – from Bosnia and Albania – were strictly separated from the Asian ones, coming from Constantinople, Persia, and Armenia. Turkish merchants brought oil, wax, raw wool, and leather to Venice, which they sold or exchanged for products from Italy and northern Europe.

In 1859, the municipality of Venice bought the palace – which by then was in desperate need of extensive repairs – and started a ten-year-long and very costly renovation. The original project was used wherever possible. The walls erected to close the building's façade were removed, a small house built on the palace's right side was demolished, and the two turrets were rebuilt, together with the crowning battlements. At work's completion, the edifice was restored in all its sixteenth-century glory. Today, the Fontego dei Turchi is home to the city's Natural History Museum.

Ca' Vendramin Calergi

Almost exactly opposite the Fontego dei Turchi, on the canal's left side, this splendid mansion houses the storied Casinò di Venezia (Venice Casino), founded in 1638, the oldest still operating casino in the world. The word *ca'* is a contraction of the Italian *casa*, which means home or house. You will find many historic mansions in Venice whose name starts with Ca' followed by a family name.

This genuinely stunning mansion is an excellent example of Venetian Renaissance architecture. Built between 1481 and 1509 for the Loredan family, a patrician family whose roots went back to the eleventh century and who gave three doges to the Republic, it was designed by architect Mauro Codussi. Codussi drew inspiration from two works by famed architect, mathematician, writer, and humanist Leon Battista Alberti – one of Renaissance architecture founders alongside Filippo Brunelleschi – to create its elaborate façade: Palazzo Rucellai in Florence and the Saint Andrew Basilica in Mantua, where Alberti had been called in 1459 by Ludovico III Gonzaga to beautify the city.

The palace's façade is on three levels, all done in white marble and lavishly decorated with an abundance of Doric, Ionic, and Corinthian columns. Two series of five mullioned windows enliven the building's two upper floors. Codussi achieved a nice contrasting effect of lights and shadows through the expert use of solids and voids. Inside, the rooms and the large staircase are mainly decorated with stucco. The public can visit several rooms on a guided tour but only by appointment through the casino.

Over the centuries, this beautiful mansion changed hands several times, ending in the possession of the Vendramin family – related to the Calergi family – in 1739. The world-famous German composer Richard Wagner spent the last two years of his life here, dying in this house on 13 February 1883. In 1946, the municipality of Venice acquired the property, making it the winter seat of its casino (all four of Italy's casinos are publicly owned). The summer seat, now closed, was a Fascist building designed by the same Eugenio Miozzi responsible for the Academy Bridge and erected in the record time of eight months in 1938 at the Lido of Venice, on the outer edge of the lagoon. In 1999, the Venice Casino opened a second, modern, unglamorous building on the mainland, near the Marco Polo airport.

Ca' Pesaro

Just a few houses away from the Fondaco of the Turks on the Grand Canal's right bank rises this majestic building, one of the city's most important palaces. Commissioned by the aristocratic and extremely wealthy Pesaro family, it was built between 1659 and 1710 on a project by architect and sculptor Baldassare Longhena, perhaps the leading figure of Venetian Baroque. When he died in February 1682, the building wasn't finished yet, but it was later completed respecting his design.

Its size, decorative quality, and grandeur make Ca' Pesaro one of Venice's best-known and significant mansions. The Baroque façade is a spectacular – if somewhat heavy – specimen of that architectural style, its play of lights and shadows obtained through protruding low reliefs and an abundance of columns on the upper floors. The diamond-shaped ashlar decoration at the building's bottom floors is eye-catching for its prominence. At the same time, seven richly decorated round arches enliven both main floors, most of them windowed, separated by columns that double in correspondence with the load-bearing walls. The entrance to the palace is through two water doors.

On the inside, allegorical frescos, low reliefs, and statues await the visitors. Unfortunately, much of the palace's impressive art collection, including works by such masters as Tintoretto, Bellini, Giorgione, Tiziano, and many of the best-known Venetian artists of the seventeenth and eighteenth centuries, was dispersed by 1830, when the last exponent of the Pesaro family died. In 1902, the Duchess Felicita Bevilacqua La Masa, Ca' Pesaro's latest owner, donated it to the municipality of Venice, which destined it to become the city's International Gallery of Modern Art and Oriental Art Museum.

Ca' d'Oro

Venice's "Golden House" – not far from Ca' Pesaro but on the canal's opposite side – was commissioned by Marino Contarini, a wealthy merchant who also tried his hand at the city's politics without much success. The mansion was completed in 1442 under the direction of two Venetian architects, the brothers Giovanni and Bartolomeo Bono, becoming the most prestigious example of Venetian late-Gothic architecture. Its name derives from the original decoration of the building's façade, a glorious polychrome with many golden finishes, now sadly gone.

Despite several changes of ownership and consequent renovation or enlargement works, the Ca' d'Oro retains much of the flair and grandeur of its original project. In 1894, Baron Giorgio Franchetti, an Italian patron and art collector, acquired the property, starting an extensive and expensive renovation to bring the palace back to its original appearance to the fullest extent possible. He aspired making the building a home for his considerable art collection, which he wished to make accessible to the public. Franchetti made a deal with the Italian State (still the Kingdom of Italy) to help with the immense renovation costs. In exchange for covering all expenses, the state would get full ownership of the building, leading to the inauguration of the Giorgio Franchetti Art Gallery at Ca' d'Oro in January 1927.

The building's façade is characterized by the asymmetry between the right and left halves. On the left side's ground floor, a portico with five big arches in the Byzantine style allows for the mooring of boats. The two upper floors are magnificent, each defined by a loggia with six arches. The marble elements look as if they were carved into a single monolith, emerging from the black void behind. On the other hand, the right side is much simpler but equally impressive, with its six arched and three square windows arising from a masonry cladding. Overall, the Ca' d'Oro well illustrates the transition from the Gothic to the Renaissance.

Ca' Foscari

Toward the final part of the Grand Canal, between the Rialto and Academy Bridges, lie three of Venice's most notable palaces, all close to one another. The first of the three coming from the north, on the waterway's right bank, is this majestic patrician residence, which now hosts the headquarters of the University of Venice, one of the most prestigious academic institutions in the country.

The mansion was built by Doge Francesco Foscari between 1453 and 1457 in late Venetian Gothic style as his private residence after demolishing the previous mansion standing in its place, called Casa delle due Torri (House of the Two Towers). That older building, done in Byzantine style, was well-known in the city thanks to its sought-after position "in the bend of the canal" and its two imposing side towers. The Republic of Venice bought it from its previous owner, Bernardo Giustinian, in 1429 to make a representative residence of it. Over the years, it housed such high-level personalities as Gianfrancesco Gonzaga, Lord of Mantua and a commanding officer in Venice's army, Francesco Sforza, Duke of Milan, King Henry III of France in 1574, Tsar Peter I (the Great) of Russia in 1698, as well as several foreign dignitaries.

The building is attributed to Venetian sculptor and architect Bartolomeo Bon, who also created the impressive Porta della Carta at Palazzo Ducale. Bon's project featured the addition of a second *piano nobile* (main floor) instead of the traditional single one and the largest private courtyard in all of Venice – at 10,000 square feet – second only to that of the Doge's Palace. Due to the mansion's desirable location and the wide-ranging view over the canal, famous painters like Giovanni Antonio Canal – known as Canaletto – Michele Marieschi, and Francesco Guardi often chose it as their preferred spot for working on their acclaimed views. Canaletto, for instance, painted both his *Canal Grande da Ca' Balbi verso Rialto* – which can be seen at the Museum of the Eighteenth Century at Ca' Rezzonico, just a few steps away – and *Regata sul Canal Grande* – part of Windsor Castle's Royal Collection – from Ca' Foscari's third floor. The building itself was depicted in several paintings.

Today's main entrance is at the building's back, where a beautiful portal made of Istrian stone is one of the palace's highlights. It is framed by checkered friezes on the outside and decorated on the inside. It is surmounted by an inflected arch lunette, occupied by the coat of arms of the House of Foscari, with the Lion of St. Mark in its top left corner. When a Napoleonic decree in 1797 abolished all coats of arms, it had to be hidden under a layer of lime, like many others in town. The main façade, overlooking the canal, is dominated by two splendidly decorated polyphorae (big eight-part windows) topped by a large stone frieze. This was originally embellished by gold and lapis lazuli decorations but was damaged upon Napoleon's arrival in town.

Palazzo Grassi

On the opposite side of Ca' Foscari, Palazzo Grassi is famous for being perhaps the last grand mansion built in Venice before the fall of the Venetian Republic and for housing one of the city's premier art museums, the Pinault Collection. The palace has had a turbulent history due to it changing hands more than once, with each new owner adapting it to their needs.

Toward the beginning of the eighteenth century, the already wealthy Grassi family acquired a noble title. Motivated by the desire to make their new social status visible to all and needing a suitable family residence worthy of their standing, they started buying as much real estate as they could between the Grand Canal, Campo San Samuele – a small square before the church of San Samuele –, and the adjacent streets. The result was a large, trapezoidal lot with a wide frontage overlooking the canal that they could use to build the immense and luxurious palace they had in mind, after tearing down all the modest houses they had taken ownership of. In 1732, the whole family clan moved into an existing building, much smaller than the eventual Palazzo Grassi but still respectable by any standard, which today is a 5-star hotel known as Palazzina Grassi, immediately to the left of the main palace.

Construction work on the new mansion began in 1748 and lasted until 1772. The Grassis commissioned a residence that had to be as awe-inspiring from the outside as it was elegant and refined on the inside. No expense was spared. Following the lot's contours, the building's plan is shaped like a trapeze, arranged around a large central courtyard. The imposing façade, primarily done in Istrian stone, is exquisite in its clean Venetian Flowery Gothic style, a far cry from its Renaissance and Baroque peers. On the inside, the grand staircase is located at the farthest point from the main entrance, forcing visitors to cross both the atrium and the courtyard, thus allowing them to appreciate the monumentality of the spaces.

After several changes in ownership, the palace was acquired in 2005 by French magnate Francois Pinault – whose family owns 42% of Kering, an international holding with controlling stakes in brands such as Gucci, Yves Saint Laurent, Bottega Veneta, Balenciaga, Alexander McQueen, Brioni, Boucheron, Pomellato, and others –, who was looking for a suitable setting to showcase his impressive private collection of modern and contemporary art. The new owner entrusted famed Japanese architect Tadao Ando with renovating the building. Ando's intervention was minimal and non-invasive, respecting the original project, mainly based on finding better ways for natural and artificial lights to make the internal spaces even more appealing. Some original fine marble details and stuccos were also restored.

Ca' Rezzonico

Ca' Rezzonico, considered one of the Grand Canal's greatest mansions, was built around the same time as Palazzo Grassi, essentially right before it. In 1649, the patrician Bon family commissioned a mansion to the city's most acclaimed architect, Baldassare Longhena, who also designed the imposing Ca' Pesaro and the beautiful Basilica of Saint Mary of Health at Punta della Dogana, among other works. Construction started in 1667, when several pre-existing buildings were torn down to make place for the new city palace but stopped soon after due to financial difficulties of the Bon family. The whole enterprise was a bit too ambitious for their possibilities, evidently.

New owners, the Della Torre-Rezzonico, a wealthy family admitted to the Venetian nobility only in 1687 upon payment of 100,000 Venetian ducats, took up the project. In 1750, Giambattista Rezzonico commissioned the mansion's completion to architect Giorgio Massari, who was very much in vogue among the rich and famous at the time. The palace was completed by 1758, just in time to celebrate the highest point reached by this family in their seemingly unstoppable social ascent: the election to St. Peter's Throne of Carlo della Torre di Rezzonico – Giambattista's brother –, from now on Pope Clement XIII (6 July 1758).

Within the following generation, though, the Rezzonicos disappeared from history. Left without any male heir, the family name died out in 1810. Over the nineteenth century, the building changed hands several times, sadly stripped of all its remarkable furnishings in the process. One of the palace's last tenants was famed composer and songwriter Cole Porter, who rented it between 1926 and 1927 for the equivalent of $70,000 a month (in 2023 US dollars) and used it to throw legendary parties under the banner of indulgent luxury and extravagance. In 1935, the municipality bought the now hollowed-out building to house its eighteenth-century art collections of paintings, furnishings, everyday objects, and frescos from other city buildings.

The palace's façade stands out for its size and monumentality. It is divided into three floors of equal proportions, with an attic on top. The ground floor, sporting ashlar decorations, has a triple water portal leading into the palace. Ten columns each enrich the two main floors, framing seven round-headed windows topped by keystones. The attic mezzanine has oval single-lancet windows that almost disappear from the façade's grand design. The building's inner courtyard is built in a way to lead the visitors' gaze directly to the family's coat of arms, placed in full light above a fountain opposite the main entrance.

CHURCHES

Like every self-respecting town in Italy, Venice is full of churches. By some accounts, over two hundred Catholic houses of worship grace the city's streets and squares, an impressive number for such a constrained space. St. Mark's Basilica aside, at least four need mentioning.

<u>Basilica di Santa Maria della Salute</u> (Saint Mary of Health)

Simply called La Salute by Venetians, this is one of Venice's most important churches. It is located at Punta della Dogana, at the very end of the Grand Canal, not far from St. Mark's Square, but on the canal's opposite side. It was built between 1631 and 1687 to thank Our Lady for ending the catastrophic plague that had decimated the city's population, killing at least 80,000 Venetians – including Doge

Nicolò Contarini and Patriarch Giovanni Tiepolo – and many more people on the mainland.

The basilica overlooks the entrance to the Grand Canal from the south. It is accessed via an imposing staircase that almost seems to emerge from the water, leading to the church's doorway. Its distinctive feature is the double dome, the bigger one representing a rosary and the smaller one intended as the actual sanctuary. The central dome is topped by a statue of the Virgin holding the staff of *Capitana de mar* (captain of the seas). The basilica's exterior is richly decorated with statues of kings and prophets from the Old Testament, such as David, Isaiah, Jeremiah, Daniel, and many others. Above the main triangular tympanum, a statue of the Virgin and Child welcomes the visitors entering the church.

The basilica's interior is vast and bright. It consists of an ample, open space under the main dome from which six side chapels are accessed. Under the minor dome, an ellipsoidal rotunda is meant to be the actual presbytery and is home to the precious and venerated image of the Madonna of Health. The whole rotunda sets the stage for the main altar, the basilica's natural centerpiece. This sanctuary, designed by Venetian architect and sculptor Baldassare Longhena and considered a masterpiece of Venetian Baroque, was raised to the status of minor basilica by Pope Benedict XV in 1921.

Basilica di San Giorgio Maggiore

San Giorgio is a church enjoying its splendid isolation on the namesake island, facing the Doge's Palace across the water. It owes its fame to a stunning façade, designed by none other than Andrea Palladio, the Venetian Renaissance architect famous for the many villas he created in the Republic's countryside – which have all been designated UNESCO World Heritage Sites – and widely considered one of the most influential personalities in the history of Western architecture. Palladio's project was carried out between 1591 and 1610 by Vincenzo Scamozzi, another prominent Venetian architect, after the master had died in 1580.

An ancient church was already present on the island in the ninth century. In 982, Doge Tribuno Memmo donated the entire island to a Benedictine monk, Giovanni Morosini, who was happy to found a monastery in that quiet place. The current, square-shaped bell tower is made of the ever-present Istrian stone and has a conical spire. The view from the top, accessible by elevator, is breathtaking. Built in 1791, after the original one had collapsed in 1774, at 245 feet in height, it is the fourth tallest in Venice.

Inside the church, two paintings by Tintoretto, one of the Republic's most celebrated artists, are the basilica's most priceless works of art: one is his version of the *Last Supper*, and the other is called *Gathering Manna*. The choir stalls are decorated with low reliefs by Albert van den Brulle, a Dutch wood engraver also responsible for a magnificent sculpture in nut wood depicting Saint George in the act of killing the dragon. The monastery's refectory was originally enriched by an enormous painting by well-known Renaissance painter Paolo Veronese – *Wedding at Cana* –, which was stolen by the French in 1797 on the orders of Napoleon and can be seen at the Louvre Museum in Paris.

In March 1900, Pope Leo XIII elevated San Giorgio to the rank of minor basilica.

Basilica di Santa Maria Gloriosa dei Frari

This church, simply *i Frari* (the Brothers) for the locals, is Venice's largest one. The rather plain exterior with terracotta cladding is an excellent example of the transition from Romanesque to Gothic architecture. It belies an interior space choke-full of beautiful works of art, such as paintings, sculptures, and funerary monuments. The church received its title of minor basilica from Pope Pius XI in 1926.

In 1231, the Minor Friars received from Doge Jacopo Tiepolo a marshland in Contrada San Stefano Confessor to drain, where they could build their monastery with the mandatory adjoining church, which they promptly did. The church they initially constructed proved to be way too small to accommodate the many believers wanting to attend the services, thus prompting the friars to build a second one starting in 1250. Eighty years later, this second church had to be expanded again, resulting in the current structure dating back to 1338. The façade, though, was only completed in 1440, and the main altar was consecrated in 1469.

The final touches to the church were only made possible by the generosity of the Pesaro family (see Ca' Pesaro above), which earned them a noble family chapel inside the sacristy and a side altar with their very own altarpiece – the *Pala Pesaro* – painted by Titian, one of Venice's most celebrated painters. Another work by the same master – the 23-foot-tall *Assunta*, depicting the Assumption of the Virgin in heaven – graces the main altar and is considered an absolute masterpiece of Venetian Renaissance, the painting definitively consecrating Titian, then in his early twenties, in the Olympus of the great masters of his time.

In total, the basilica accommodates seventeen monumental altars, as well as countless works of art and several funerary monuments, among them those of Titian himself and the one belonging to Antonio Canova, the sculptor and painter universally regarded as the most prominent exponent of Neoclassicism.

Chiesa di San Zaccaria

This church, another of Venice's gems, is dedicated to Saint Zachary. According to the Biblical account, Zachary was a Jewish priest in Jerusalem who, as an elderly man, was still childless (which, by the way, was considered shameful in that culture). His wife,

Elizabeth, was beyond childbearing age. Yet, an angel told him in a vision that they would have a son and that they should call him John. This would be John the Baptist, the preacher who would baptize Jesus in the river Jordan years later.

The first church on this site dates to the ninth century, when Byzantium's Emperor Leo V the Armenian donated the supposed remains of St. Zachary to Venice to strengthen the friendly relations between the two powers. A Benedictine monastery was also added near the church, but both were destroyed in 1105 by a devastating fire that claimed the lives of some one hundred nuns, who were asphyxiated after seeking shelter in the basement. It is said that Pope Benedict III took refuge in the monastery in 855 to escape the violence unleashed against him by the antipope Anastasius III.

The history of the current church began in 1458, under Doge Pasquale Malipiero, when the Benedictine nuns commissioned architects Antonio Gambello and Mauro Codussi to design a new place of worship worthy of the history of their order. The result is sometimes referred to as a "pearl casket," whose most prominent feature is, without a doubt, the elegant, Renaissance-style façade. Almost wholly done in Istrian stone, it is divided into three parts by ascending pillars and columns and lightened by several tall and slender windows. On the very top of the façade, which is decorated with sculptures and low reliefs, the statue of St. Zachary welcomes visitors.

The church's interior, divided into three naves,

houses several artistic treasures. Among them, the altarpiece by Giovanni Bellini, one of the greatest Venetian painters ever and among the most famous Renaissance artists, is an undisputed masterpiece of Renaissance art. It is called *Sacra Conversazione* (*Holy Conversation*), or simply Pala di San Zaccaria, and is placed in a niche above the altar on the left wall. It depicts the Virgin with Child seated on the throne, with four saints around her. From left to right, they are St. Peter, St. Catherine of Alexandria, St. Lucia, and St. Jerome.

Located in a small square not far from St. Mark's and the Doge's Palace, this church should be part of every visitor's itinerary.

* * *

Churches worth a visit in this unique city are too many to count. To visit most of them, there's an entrance fee of €3. If you wish to see more than four, it might be advisable to buy a cumulative ticket called Chorus Pass, which is sold in any of the participating churches and online and costs €12, giving access to fifteen of the best-known ones (but none of the four presented here).

SCUOLA GRANDE DI SAN ROCCO

The Great School of Saint Roch is a must-see for every art lover. Located just behind the Basilica dei Frari, this impressive Renaissance building houses an incredible array of artistic masterpieces, making it an unmissable stop for every first-time visitor to Venice. The School was founded in 1478 as a school of devotion by a fraternity of *Battuti*, a lay confraternity engaged in charitable and socially beneficial work of various kinds. In 1489, after receiving from the Franciscan friars nearby part of their cemetery for free, they started building their church, which stands on the right of the main building's façade. It was consecrated in 1508 and is dedicated to St. Roch, whose relic had been brought to Venice in 1485.

After the church, it was time to build the fraternity's headquarters. Works on the new, exquisite building began in 1517, and the School was complete by 1560. The building's façade is a triumph of columns, fine decoration, colored marble, and porphyry. All columns are fluted and surrounded by garlands – similar to the nearby church – of vines, laurel, and oak. The columns' bases are decorated with lying animals, including a tiny elephant, which is peculiar.

In 1564, thanks to its growing wealth and prestige, the fraternity could hire Tintoretto, one of Venice's greatest painters, to decorate the School's interior, transforming it into a veritable museum of his art. When he was done twenty-four years later, his cycle of large canvasses spread over three rooms rapidly gained it the title of "Sistine Chapel of Venice." Among the many wonderful paintings, his world-famous, gigantic *Crucifixion* towers over all else, part of a cycle about the Passion of Jesus Christ. The chapter room's ceiling and walls are plastered with a stunning showcase of the great master's unparalleled skills. Among a long list of masterpieces, *Saint Roch in glory*, *Moses drawing water from the rock*, *Ascension*, *Flight into Egypt*, *Baptism of Christ*, *Circumcision*, and *Ascent to Calvary* stand out, divided between the chapter room and the *sala terrena*, the School's passage hall. An *Annunciation* by Titian, another of the giants of art history, is just as good and valuable.

Not to be outdone, the nearby church also contains a long list of beautiful works of art, some by Tintoretto himself or his workshop staff. The Scuola Grande di San Rocco is still active today, with its three hundred brothers continuing the charitable mission for which it was created.

MURANO

The island of Murano, which is, in fact, a group of five small islets separated by canals, like everything else in Venice, is the world-renowned center of artistic glass, whose tradition dates to the thirteenth century, reaching its maximum splendor in the fifteenth and sixteenth centuries.

On the island, formerly called Amuriana, the inhabited center developed in the Lombard period with the influx of refugees from the mainland, and since then, it has been governed by its own magistrates (tribunes); in the twelfth century, it was incorporated into the Santa Croce district of Venice. The Republic sent a podestà – a chief magistrate or mayor – there in 1271 and always respected its autonomous set of rules (with a major and a minor council).

The Basilica of Saints Mary and Donato dates to the seventh century but was rebuilt in the twelfth. It contains mosaics from the twelfth and thirteenth centuries and fourteenth-century altarpieces. On the outside, Lombard forms and Oriental decorative elements blend.

On the island, there are many laboratories and ancient factories where it is possible to learn about the age-old techniques used in the blown glass manufacturing process, handed down from generation to generation throughout the centuries. Visitors can buy the original Murano glass in many forms and shapes. Please be advised that items are never cheap and that an object signed by the artisan and accompanied by a certificate of authenticity is worth much more than an unsigned one.

The Museum of Murano Glass on the island is well worth a visit, too.

THE JEWISH GHETTO

Venice's Jewish ghetto is the oldest one ever established on Italian soil. On 29 March 1516, the Republic's Senate decreed that all the Jews present in town had to be segregated from the rest of the population, thus creating the *ghetto* (a word indicating a special district reserved for the Jewish population in many European cities). Before the establishment of the ghetto in Venice, most Jews lived on the Venetian mainland, with very few families residing in the lagoon. They worked mainly as moneylenders and merchants, and some even practiced the medical art, but they were excluded from any corporation – or guild – and were not allowed to own real estate. They could stay in the city for no longer than fifteen consecutive days, plying their trade at the Rialto market, before having to return to the mainland.

After the disastrous Battle of Agnadello on 14 May 1509, where the troops of the League of

Cambrai under the leadership of King Louis XII of France decisively defeated the Venetian Republic, expelling it from all territories in the Lombardy region, Venice found itself in dire social and financial straits. Hence was born the idea of allowing Jews to reside in its historic center in exchange for a yearly remittance of 6,500 ducats per family. Many of them started settling in the Rialto area, which angered residents, prompting the Senate to segregate them into a secluded area – the ghetto. To house all Jews residing in the city, the district of Cannaregio was chosen north of the Santa Lucia train station. High walls surrounded the ghetto; the doors opened at dawn and closed again in the evening. Guards, paid for from the Jews' own money, monitored the enclosure and roamed the surrounding canals.

The district is rendered unique by the presence of no less than five synagogues, the Spanish one being the biggest and best-known, two of which are accessible to visitors. All religious and administrative institutions of Venice's Jewish community are in the ghetto to this day. This is a fascinating district to visit, and every traveler coming to Venice should experience its unique atmosphere, learning about the history, customs, and traditions of the Jews in Venice in the process.

THE VENICE FILM FESTIVAL

The Mostra Internazionale d'Arte Cinematografica – its full name – had its first edition in 1932 as part of the much older Biennale di Venezia, the cultural foundation that organizes the biannual International Art Exhibition in Venice. It originated from a project by Count Giuseppe Volpi di Misurata (Misrata, in Libya), then the Biennale's president, the sculptor Antonio Maraini, and the film critic Luciano De Feo. Benito Mussolini, Fascist Italy's Duce, was immediately sold on the idea, which he considered an excellent way of disseminating Italian culture in the world through the new means of cinematography, at the same time enhancing his regime's prestige on the international scene.

The Venice Film Festival thus became the first of its kind, well ahead of the Cannes Film Festival in France – established in 1946 – and the Berlin Film Festival in Germany – established in 1951. On 6 August 1932, the first movie ever in the history of the festival – *Dr. Jekyll and Mr. Hyde*, directed by Rouben Mamoulian – was screened on the terrace of the Hotel Excelsior at the Lido of Venice, followed by a grand ball in the hotel's lounges. Count Volpi's role in the festival's birth is reflected in the name of the prize awarded to actors and actresses for the best performance, which is called Coppa Volpi (Volpi Cup) to this day. The festival's highest prize for the best film is the Golden Lion.

Count Giuseppe Volpi was an important figure in Italian politics. The son of a construction engineer, after his father's premature death, he abandoned his university studies and went into business. As a sales representative, he met the financial circles linked to the Banca Commerciale and, with its support, was able to promote economic activities in the Far East and the Balkans. In Italy, he founded the Adriatic Electricity Company, destined to become one of the country's most influential industrial groups. He planned the construction of the port of Marghera on the mainland before Venice (1919). He then was nominated governor of Tripolitania, an Italian colony encompassing Libya's northwestern regions (1921-25). Misrata, in fact, is a city on the Libyan coast east of Tripoli. As Minister of Finance (1925-29), he regulated war debts and inaugurated a policy to increase state control over the economy. In December 1927, he signed the law stabilizing the lira, the so-called Quota 90. He was a senator and member of the Grand Council of Fascism. As such, he was arrested by the Germans after Italy's armistice with the Allies. Once freed, he fled to Switzerland, returning to Italy in 1947.

Every year, Hollywood royalty descend on Venice to bask in the adulation of their fans, smile for the cameras, sail the city's channels, and participate in the celebrations surrounding the event. Oh, and they present their latest films, too.

MUSEUMS

Venice has about forty museums, most of them housed in stunning mansions that are themselves worth a visit. Here are the ten most notable ones:

Gallerie dell'Accademia

The Accademia galleries are the world's most valuable and complete gallery of Venetian paintings between the fourteenth and eighteenth centuries. Since 1807, they have been located within a complex of three buildings: the Scuola Grande della Carità, the Church of Santa Maria della Carità, and the Convent of the Lateran Canons, a building by Palladio. In its rooms, visitors will find a fascinating collection of paintings that provides a complete picture of the Venetian school spanning five centuries, from the Medieval and Byzantine periods to the Baroque, passing through the Renaissance. Some of the masterpieces of several great masters, such as Bellini, Giorgione, Mantegna, Titian, Tintoretto, Veronese, and Tiepolo, are kept here.

Peggy Guggenheim Collection

The Peggy Guggenheim Collection is one of the world's most prestigious modern art museums, comprising hundreds of twentieth-century European and American works of art. It is based in Palazzo Venier dei Leoni, a beautiful eighteenth-century villa with a big garden overlooking the Grand Canal that once was Peggy Guggenheim's home. Ms. Guggenheim was a heiress and art collector whose father died in the sinking of the Titanic (1912) when she was only 14. Her great love for the avant-garde of the twentieth century, from Abstraction to Futurism, made it possible to create one of the richest collections in the sector, including the great masterpieces of artists the likes of Umberto Boccioni, Marc Chagall, Salvador Dalì, René Magritte, Amedeo Modigliani, Pablo Picasso, Andy Warhol, and many more. The museum houses not only Peggy Guggenheim's personal collection but also significant works from the Hannelore B. and Rudolph B. Schulhof Collection, the Patsy R. and Raymond D. Nasher Sculpture Garden, and many temporary exhibitions.

Marciana National Library

The most ancient and important library in Venice, the Marciana – which roughly translates to St. Mark's Library – is an awe-inspiring container for a cultural heritage of inestimable value. One of the most prestigious libraries in Italy and Europe, it is housed inside a magnificent building designed by famed sixteenth-century architect and sculptor Jacopo Sansovino, overlooking the San Marco basin and made more noteworthy thanks to works by Titian, Veronese, and Tintoretto. Inside, there are more than 600,000 printed books and 10,000 manuscripts, including one of the most valuable collections of Greek, Latin, and Oriental manuscripts in the world. There is also an extensive collection of geographical maps and atlases. The library is still functioning as an important study and research center. Guided tours can access several public spaces, such as the monumental staircase, the vestibule, and the hall, where pictorial masterpieces decorate the walls.

International Gallery of Modern Art at Ca' Pesaro

In 1899, Duchess Bevilacqua La Masa, the building's last owner, donated the residence of Ca' Pesaro (see above) to the city of Venice so that it could become the site of a permanent art exhibition for young artists. Venice's new Gallery of Modern Art was inaugurated in 1902. It now houses paintings and sculptures from the nineteenth and twentieth centuries, including masterpieces by Gustav Klimt, Marc Chagall, Joan Miró, Vasilij Kandinsky, Paul Klee, Henri Matisse, and Henry Moore, as well as a permanent exhibition of works by Italian artists, such as Felice Casorati, Mario Sironi, Giorgio Morandi, and Giorgio De Chirico. The gallery offers an exhibition itinerary along the ten rooms on the first floor of the building, which in recent years has been completely renovated in its layout, offering a suggestive key to understanding the evolution of this historical-artistic period. The second floor is home to temporary exhibitions.

Oriental Art Museum at Ca' Pesaro

Also housed at Ca' Pesaro, on the higher floor, is the Museum of Oriental Art, encompassing a collection of thousands of art objects and examples of fine craftsmanship put together by Prince Henry of Bourbon, who between 1887 and 1889 visited China, Japan, Indonesia, and other parts of Southeastern Asia, purchasing over 30,000 pieces. This museum was inaugurated in 1929, and it displays the most extensive collection of Oriental art in all of Europe. The Japanese sector enjoys great fame for its large number of pieces from the Edo period (1603-1867).

Naval History Museum

In a city like Venice, entirely dependent on naval

power for its wealth and historical importance, how could a museum not be dedicated to maritime history? The Naval History Museum, owned by the Italian Navy, is an unmissable visit for anyone wanting to experience the deep bond between Venice and the seas directly. The main seat is a fifteenth-century building once used as a granary; near the entrance to the naval arsenal, the ancient workshop is home to the captivating Ships Pavilion. The display includes models of Venetian fortresses along the Adriatic and Aegean Seas, reconstructions of war galleys, historic gondolas, and model ships from all over the world.

Museo del Settecento at Ca' Rezzonico

The Museum of the Eighteenth Century of Venice is housed in the majestic palace of Ca' Rezzonico on the Grand Canal, designed by architects Longhena and Massari and now owned by the municipality of Venice (see above). Among the precious furnishings of the time, the museum houses works of inestimable value from the Venetian eighteenth century, created by artists such as Tiepolo, Longhi, Guardi, and Canaletto. The visit begins from the large staircase designed by Massari. Then, it develops on the first floor through eleven rooms, where it is possible to admire paintings, sculptures, frescos, and eighteenth-century furnishings. In the Brustolon Room, some of the greatest masterpieces of Venetian carving of the early eighteenth century are exhibited. On the second floor, seventeenth-century paintings dominated by two canvases by Canaletto welcome visitors, followed by a room dedicated to the work of Longhi and the frescos by Tiepolo taken from Villa Zianigo. On the third floor, there is the Egidio Martini Art Gallery, with around three hundred works, almost all of the Venetian school, dating from the fifteenth century to the beginning of the twentieth century. Finally, the Browning Mezzanine houses the Mestrovich Collection, with important works by artists such as Tintoretto and Bonifacio de' Pitati.

Palazzo Grassi

Palazzo Grassi (see above) is an acclaimed Venetian museum center with large international exhibitions. Built between 1748 and 1772 by architect Giorgio Massari, it is the last great neoclassical-inspired palace built on the Grand Canal before the fall of the Republic of Venice. In 1840, the Grassi family sold the palace, which subsequently passed through several owners before hosting the International Center of Arts and Costume in 1951. Taken over in 1983 by the Fiat Group and restored by Italian star architect Gae Aulenti, it has become one of Europe's most prestigious exhibition centers, featuring big art and archeology exhibitions. Since 2005, the building has been owned by French tycoon and art collector François Pinault, who entrusted the reorganization of the spaces to another star architect, the Japanese Tadao Ando, known for his minimalist taste. The museum reopened to the public in 2006 with an exhibition showcasing Pinault's extensive collection of contemporary and modern art for the first time.

Natural History Museum

In 1923, the Fontego dei Turchi (see above), after being the old Correr Museum seat for a while, became home to Venice's Natural History Museum. Its collection includes two million pieces, covering approximately seven hundred million years. There are zoological, entomological, and botanical collections to see, and there's an entire section dedicated to paleontology. On the ground floor, the Cetacean Gallery, with the skeleton of a whale and a young sperm whale, and the Tegnùe Aquarium, rich in marine species and invertebrates, are much-beloved highlights. A scientific library completes the museum.

Correr Museum

In 1830, right before dying, Venetian nobleman Teodoro Correr donated his impressive art collection to the city of Venice. It was initially housed in the Fontego dei Turchi before being transferred to the Procuratie Nuove in St. Mark's Square in 1922. The Correr Museum is divided into three sections: the Historical Collections, the Picture Gallery, and the Museum of the Risorgimento – the time when Italy's identity as an independent nation was formed in the nineteenth century.

From the same author

Rome – Its History, Its Art, Its Landmarks

Athens – Its History, Its Art, Its Landmarks

Florence – Its History, Its Art, Its Landmarks

Italy's Finest – Rome, Venice, Florence (Omnibus edition)

Las Vegas The Grand – The Strip, the Casinos, the Mob, the Stars

Made in United States
Troutdale, OR
03/21/2024